P9-CEV-898

4° | Introduction

9 | **ADVENT WEEK ONE: BE READY**
Sunday: *Reactions to Change*
Monday-Saturday

31 | **ADVENT WEEK TWO: BE FRUITFUL**
Sunday: *Do as I Say, Not as I Do*
Monday-Saturday

57 | **ADVENT WEEK THREE: BE BLESSED**
Sunday: *Expectations*
Monday-Saturday

83 | **ADVENT WEEK FOUR: BE AMAZED**
Sunday: *Be Amazed*
Monday-Tuesday

93 | **Christmas Day**

96 | Notes

Celebrate...

They will call him **Immanuel** (which means **"God with us"**).

—Matthew 1:23b

Celebrate...

This intermediate coming is like a road on which we travel from his first coming to his last. In the first, Christ was our redemption; in the last, he will appear as our life; in his intermediate coming, he is our comfort and our rest. —St. Bernard of Clairvaux[1]

The Advents

Advent is a Latin word that literally means "coming" or "appearing." The word leads us to remember how Jesus, God's Messiah, first came to us. The word also reminds us that Jesus told us, "My Father's house has many rooms; if that were not so, would I have told you that I am going there to prepare a place for you? And if I go and prepare a place for you, I will come back and take you to be with me that you also may be where I am" (John 14:2-3).

But Advent is more than just preparing for Christmas and waiting for the return of the Lord. There is an intermediate Advent. Through the sending out of the Spirit by the Father and the Son, the Spirit of Christ is in our midst. The Spirit who is our *Paraclete*, which means Comforter, takes up residence in our hearts as we turn from our way of life and are made new in Christ. The Spirit of Christ is hidden within the life of the Church, as it is sent out on God's mission. Jesus says, "If you love me, keep my commands. And I will ask the Father, and he will give you another advocate to help you and be with you forever" (John 14:15-16).

celebrate

An Advent Experience

Paul Sheneman

BEACON HILL PRESS
OF KANSAS CITY

Copyright 2013 by Beacon Hill Press of Kansas City

ISBN: 978-0-8341-3049-4

Printed in the
United States of America

Cover: Lindsey McCormack

In the intermediate, the Church witnesses to the reality that the Spirit of Christ comes to us now. As the Church goes out to do and speak the good news of the kingdom of God, the Spirit of Christ is seen working and moving within those who call themselves Christ-followers. As we travel the road to Advent season, the presence of Christ being made known in our world is reason to celebrate.

Celebrate

Often Christmas is envisioned as a time for celebrating. To celebrate can mean to engage in festivities, which is often what is meant when we say, "We're looking forward to celebrating Christmas." Taking a break, spending time with family, singing, feasting, and giving gifts are signs of the joyous Christmas festivities. Yet we often do not realize that Advent itself is a time for celebration.

We do not celebrate in Advent like we do in Christmastide. Celebrate can also mean to perform or participate in a sacrament, such as when we celebrate Communion or baptism. A sacrament is not merely an outward sign of an inward grace. A sacrament is also a means of grace. When we participate and practice a means of grace, God can and often does reveal himself through it. In short, Advent is a means of grace in which we participate. Thomas Merton put it this way, "Advent is the 'sacrament' of the presence of God in His world, in the Mystery of Christ at work in History.... This mystery is the revelation of God Himself in His Incarnate Son. But it is not merely a manifestation of the Divine, it is the concrete plan of God for the salvation of men and the restoration of the whole world in Christ."[2]

How is it that we participate in "the presence of God in His world"?

The Church, the body of Christ, goes into the world participating in the reality that God has come, is coming, and will come at the end by loving our neighbor as ourselves and proclaiming the good news of the kingdom of God. As we care for the least of these and testify to the reality of God's reign in our life together, the Church reveals the reality that our God comes. Our God shows up where there is death and brings life. We participate by God's grace in pointing people to the One who can free them from the prison of sin. As we are merciful to all we participate in the Advent.

Acts of Mercy

God's love is talked about in several different ways throughout the Scriptures. Mercy is the aspect of God's love that is revealed in God's care for the poor. This is seen in God's choosing of the weak to be His agents of restoration, His commands to care for the orphan and widow, the protection of foreigners, and the command to love your neighbor as yourself. God's love is also revealed as grace when God forgives the guilty. So mercy is merely an expression of God's love for all people and His creation.

God expected that His chosen people were to be people of mercy. Throughout the Old and New Testament God emphasizes that Israel and the Church are to act mercifully by caring for the poor and weak. In a poignant way, the prophet Micah teaches us that God desires us to be a people of mercy above any faithless religious sacrifices we may make. The prophet writes, "He has shown you, O mortal, what is good. And what does the LORD require of you? To act justly and to love mercy and to walk humbly with your God" (Micah 6:8).

In emphasizing the significance of the works of mercy and echoing the prophet Micah, Wesley wrote,

> Thus should he show his zeal for works of piety; but much more for works of mercy; seeing "God will have mercy and not sacrifice," that is, rather than sacrifice. Whenever, therefore, one interferes with the other, works of mercy are to be preferred. Even reading, hearing, prayer are to be omitted, or to be postponed, "at charity's almighty call;" when we are called to relieve the distress of our neighbour, whether in body or soul.[3]

Wesley emphasized the acts of mercy not to degrade works of piety but to point out that love of God and neighbor are at the center of what our faith is all about. To emphasize loving our neighbors is to emphasize the love of God and vise versa. Thus, acts of mercy reveal our true motivation. As Bernard of Clairvaux writes, "He who fears God will do good, but something further has been said about the one who loves, that is, that he will keep God's word. Where is God's word to be kept? Obviously in the heart, as the prophet says: I have hidden your words in my heart, so that I may not sin against you."[4] And the "word" that Bernard is referring to is both God's Word (Scripture) and *the* Word of God (Jesus Christ).

The Advent Experience: An Advent Calendar with a Twist

Advent this year begins on December 1. So there are 24 days from the start of Advent until Christmas, making the use of the popular Advent calendar an appropriate practice. But this will not be like the common children's Advent calendars that count down the days until Christmas with little toys and treats. *Instead of getting something, our aim is to give something.* We're inviting you to fill your Advent calendar with daily acts of mercy.

Each day there are three acts of mercy from which you can choose. You will see some symbols beside the acts. Here is what they mean:

- 🐾   BETTER TOGETHER: consider doing as a family, small group, or whole church

- ✉   WELCOMED WORDS: consider leaving a "Celebrate Acts of Mercy" card or note that explains the gesture

- \$ SACRIFICE TO SPEND: consider giving up something in order to be able to donate money

- ★   COMMENDABLE CHARITY: the organization has the highest rating for fiscal transparency and responsibility according to Charity Navigator

Consider making an Advent calendar as a family. Then, each time your family participates in an act of mercy, take a pen/marker and write this act on the date. If your family doesn't have time to create a calendar, visit www.adventexperience to download a full color calendar that your family can use throughout the Advent experience.

Select activities that are feasible for your week, or use them as idea starters to create your own. Sundays' acts are focused on reflection, witnessing, and prayer. Monday through Saturday's acts challenge us to care for the hungry, thirsty, stranger, naked, sick and imprisoned. This will be done in obedience to Christ (Matthew 25:31-46).

We take these daily actions throughout the Advent season to participate in the reality that our God came, is coming, and will come again. And so we will celebrate the reality that our God is the God who comes. As Thomas Merton once said, "He comes as a physician to heal the wounds of sin. He comes as a little one lest we be terrified... His Advent is less a coming than a manifestation of His presence."[5]

Each day, if possible, take time to gather your family together to read the Scripture and devotional for that day. Make this a special time of opening God's Word, sharing thoughts and feelings, and praying together. The devotionals, readings, and other materials are all designed to help you enter more deeply into specific faith practices so that you can grow in God's grace. If you have time to do all the daily devotions and readings, that's great. But if not, that's okay too. We want you to use this as a means of God's grace for your family in a way that works best. We want you and your family to be free to enter fully into the Advent experience.

SUNDAY – DAY 1

Reflection on Matthew 24:36-44

So you also must **be ready,** because the Son of Man will come at an hour when you do not expect him. (Matthew 24:44)

Reactions to Change

News of the impending merger leaked to the company before it was intended. Mike and Terrance, two mid-level managers, caught wind of it from their director. Both guys reacted to the news in completely different ways.

Mike immediately began speculating about the coming changes. The company they were merging with was known for its great customer service. Mike imagined they would cut his customer service team. He began calculating how to absorb the added workload during the transition. He imagined which employees he would have to let go first and how he should let them know. He assumed that the most obvious time for the change would be the end of the month and a strategy would have to be in place within the week. Mike cut back on current projects in order to create a transition strategy.

Terrance thought about the upcoming transition but did not let it affect day-to-day operations. He imagined that the changes would be announced in the coming days. He planned to participate in the changes as they were announced and as the implications became clear to him. He knew that he had several high-priority projects, so he kept his team working diligently toward their objectives.

A Change is Coming

Today's gospel passage is the transition in a discourse on the second coming of Jesus Christ. The first half of the discourse addresses the predictions associated with the impending change. As with any change there are signs that it is about to happen. In the case of the second coming, Jesus teaches broadly what those signs will be. The second half of the discourse addresses what it means to faithfully

watch and prepare. It gives specific directions for how we should live between the first and second Advents. In summary, the first half is about speculating and the second half is about participating.

The transition passage offers this instruction: Don't bother yourself with trying to speculate, but be about the business of participating. No one, not even the Son of God, will know the actual date and time of the second coming except for God the Father. The time will come when you least expect it. It will be like the people in the day of Noah who went around unaware until one day when the rains started to pour. So instead of imagining when and how Jesus will return, or acting as though we don't know He's coming back, we need to be prepared at all times. Like a person who knows that a thief will be breaking in but doesn't know the actual time, we must be ready!

Be Ready

Being ready requires active participation. It is not about sitting and watching out the window as though you were some type of night watchman who is on the lookout for evildoers and pranksters. Being ready is about faithfully living out the way of Jesus here and now. The return of our Lord is an activity that compels us to do good, love our neighbor as ourselves, and live as though the inbreaking of God's kingdom is already occurring.

Today's gospel passage is part of a larger discourse that tells us how to participate. Specifically, at the end of Matthew 25, Jesus tells this compelling story about the final judgment that will occur when the Son of Man comes in His glory: God will separate all people into the sheep or goat category. Then the King will say, "Come, you who are blessed by my Father; take your inheritance, the kingdom prepared for you since the creation of the world. For I was hungry and you gave me something to eat, I was thirsty and you gave me something to drink, I was a stranger and you invited me in . . ." (vv. 34-45).

The point is that we, the body of Christ, are to busy ourselves with caring for the least. The poorest of the poor are our responsibility. We are to serve those who are in all types of bondage. We are to act mercifully, for our God desires mercy and not empty religious acts. For when we serve the least of these, we are serving the Lord (v. 40).

We can celebrate in the here and now because we can witness to all people, whose lives we touch, that we serve a merciful God.

Acts of Piety

- Journal about your expectations for this Advent season.

- Testify in church, or on social networks, about a time when God used someone to be His hands and feet to you.

- Pray for the hungry, thirsty, strangers, exploited, sick, and imprisoned. Pray also that God would open your eyes to ways to help them.

MONDAY – DAY 2 – BE READY

Daily Psalm

> *Worship the LORD with gladness;*
> *come before him with joyful songs.*
> *Know that the LORD is God.*
> *It is he who made us, and we are his;*
> *we are his people, the sheep of his pasture.*
> *Enter his gates with thanksgiving*
> *and his courts with praise;*
> *give thanks to him and praise his name.*
> (Psalm 100:2-4)

Acts of Mercy

- Clip grocery coupons (online or from Sunday's paper) and put them beside the items at the store. (✉)

- Take a home-cooked meal to a family in need.

- Fast a meal and donate the money ($) to **Nazarene Compassionate Ministries Global Hunger Fund** (★). Visit http://ncm.org/projects/acm1191 for more information.

Family Devotional

Read Matthew 25:31-46.

Advent is filled with activity. Family, work, school, friends, and acquaintances enjoy our attention in varying degrees during this season. Most of these activities are a quest to fulfill the answer to a simple question, *What do you want for Christmas?* Often, greed and want seem to drive our activities during the Advent season. From crazy shopping assaults to the ungrateful acceptance of that disappointing Christmas gift, we see the darkness that our greed creates.

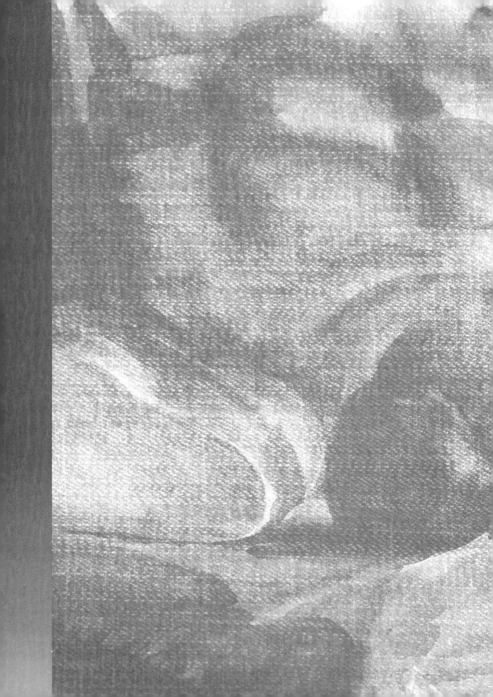

On the second day of Advent, we stop and take account of the road ahead. There are 23 days left until Christmas. There are parties and shopping. There are projects to complete, tests to take, cookies to bake, friends to visit, and the list could go on and on. So we stop here to ask ourselves if we are ready to enter into Advent. Not the kind of Advent season seeking to fulfill wants. Rather our passage today raises an important question for this Advent season, *Are we ready to serve people's needs?*

The word to separate (*aphorizo* in Greek) can mean to divide, as it clearly does in this passage. The Son of Man will divide all nations into two groups. But the word to separate also means to set apart for some purpose, and clearly can mean that here. The people were set apart into the two groups in order for the Son of Man, who is the Eternal King, to judge them. But this setting apart is not just at the end. We are set apart in Christ Jesus now. We are set apart in order to do good works that God has prepared for us. We are set apart to serve the needs of people. We are set apart to proclaim good news to the poor. The good news in the passage is manifested by our acts of mercy.

Our gospel passage today presents us with a question that will set us apart this Advent season, *Are you merely fulfilling wants or are you serving the needs of the least?* If we are daring enough to stop and ponder this question each morning, it may revolutionize our Advent experience.

Prayer
Merciful Father, amidst the chaos of the season, help us to focus on the needs of those around us and to fulfill them as an expression of our love for you. Amen.

TUESDAY – DAY 3 – BE READY

Daily Psalm

They feast on the abundance of your house;
*   you give them drink from your river of delights.*
For with you is the fountain of life;
*   in your light we see light.*
Continue your love to those who know you,
*   your righteousness to the upright in heart.*
(Psalm 36:8-10)

Acts of Mercy

• Buy a bottled drink for someone who looks thirsty (homeless, construction worker, mail carrier, police officer, bus driver). (✉)

• Set **Ripple** as your homepage and click on **WaterAid** daily. Forward the link to friends and request that they do the same. Visit http://www.ripple.org for more information.

• Donate bottled water to a local disaster relief agency or funds to support disaster relief through the **American Red Cross.** (🐾) Visit http://www.redcross.org for more information.

Family Devotional

Read 1 Thessalonians 5:1-11.

Light and dark are symbols that go to the very beginning of the church. Light was understood to be the image of righteousness, life, and justice. Dark was an image of immorality, death and injustice. We wake up to light. We conduct our daily business in the daylight. We can clearly see all that is going on in the light. But in the dark, we can hide our misdeeds. (Typically people conduct illegal or immoral activities in the cloak of darkness.)

So when the apostle Paul commands the church in Thessalonica to be awake and sober, they knew exactly what he meant. They lived in a time of persecution. The local government and economic system didn't support their new faith in the Messiah, Jesus. The local religion was not favorable to the church. Immorality and injustices in relation to their new way of life in Christ were a common part of their city. The church in Thessalonica knew that Paul's instruction was not going to be easily followed, in fact, they would suffer for it.

At times, we can't see the subtleness of the darkness because it sometimes tries to masquerade as light. The joyous feeling of giving may actually mask the sobering thought that we are gluttons. The extravagance we pour onto our loved ones this season may be a cover for the guilt we feel for not being around.

To the church at Thessalonica, and to us as well, the apostle Paul says let's put on faith, hope and love. Let us be faithful to Jesus who lived and died so that we will never be separated from Him. Let us move out each day hoping in God's ultimate future, which is the glorious return of Jesus and restoration of all things to harmony. And finally, let us move out in loving actions to our neighbor as a witness to the God who is love.

Prayer

Daystar, whose light pierces the darkest night, shine on us that we might spread your love and light to those in darkness. We ask this in the power of your Spirit. Amen.

WEDNESDAY – DAY 4 – BE READY

Daily Psalm

> Create in me a pure heart, O God,
>   and renew a steadfast spirit within me.
> Do not cast me from your presence
>   or take your Holy Spirit from me.
> Restore to me the joy of your salvation
>   and grant me a willing spirit, to sustain me.
> Then I will teach transgressors your ways,
>   so that sinners will turn back to you.
>   (Psalm 51:10-13)

Acts of Mercy

- Hug someone you normally wouldn't.

- Invite neighbors over for dessert or host a Christmas party for your neighbors (both those you know and don't know).

- Babysit for a Mommies' Day Out or Date Night Childcare event (🍲) at your church for donations to the **Dave Thomas Foundation for Adoption** (★). Visit http://www.davethomasfoundation.org/ for more information.

Family Devotional

Read Matthew 25:1-13.

Have you ever put off things until the last minute? It is common during the Advent season for the to-do lists to stack up and the obligations to mount. You quickly begin to feel like you are barely keeping up. In order to cope, prioritizing the to-do list is essential and putting things off is necessary. In the midst of all your responsibility, you might feel like the Advent season is another obligation. So when is the right time to enter into the practice of Advent?

The parable today gives us an answer. As the ten virgins are waiting for the bridegroom to come, five foolish ones do not bring enough oil to keep their lamps lit; while five wise virgins bring a back-up supply. All of them fell asleep waiting up for the bridegroom who was delayed. And then at the last minute, the five foolish ones run to get more oil because the bridgegroom's arrival is upon them.

The wise virgins in the story teach us that now is the right time to get ready. But it doesn't mean to grab your lamp and oil and jump into the Advent experience. Some speculate that the oil represents faith. Others believe it could be good works. While both of these are good options, it actually might be both. In other words, the oil may represent the whole of the life of a disciple of Jesus. Thus, faith and good works would be included.

This illustration means that as wise followers of Christ we hope for the quick return, but faithfully live not knowing the day or hour. So we must never tire of doing acts of mercy. You're invited to begin now. The reality is, if we wait until December 24 we'll miss the gift of the Advent season.

Prayer

Oh God our Strength, who breaks the bow and shatters the spear, help us persist in serving others as we wait for your eternal restoration. In Jesus Christ we pray. Amen.

THURSDAY – DAY 5 – BE READY

Daily Psalm

Trust in the Lord and do good;
   dwell in the land and enjoy safe pasture.
Take delight in the Lord,
   and he will give you the desires of your heart.
Commit your way to the Lord;
   trust in him and he will do this:
He will make your righteous reward shine like the dawn,
   your vindication like the noonday sun.
                  (Psalm 37:3-6)

Acts of Mercy

- Tape dollar bills on socks at the dollar store. (✉)

- Leave packages of wipes or diapers on the changing table in a public restroom. (✉)

- Volunteer to clean at a local rescue mission or homeless shelter. (💬)

Family Devotional

Read Luke 12:35-40.

David Wilson may not be famous; but to 1,000 customers at a K-Mart in Laguna Beach, California he became a "God-Send" prior to Christmas in 2011. David called the store and requested the amount of all the layaway charges totaling under $100. He then proceeded to write a check for almost $16,000. He became known as the Layaway Angel. David Wilson is what was known in the New Testament period as a benefactor. He gave from his greater amount of resources to clients, those with fewer resources, and K-Mart acted as the broker of that relationship.

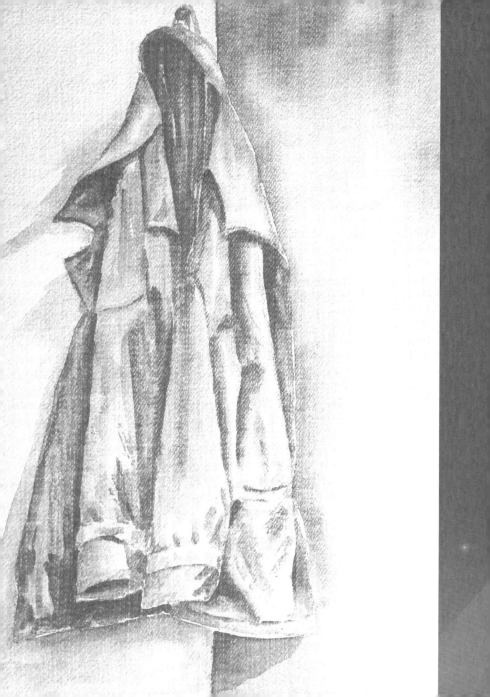

In our passage, God is portrayed as the great benefactor. He has given charge to us, His servants, the great responsibility and honor to manage His kingdom. The broker of this relationship is Jesus Christ. Though His role is not mentioned in our passage today, it is a role that Luke points out again and again throughout the gospel.

But an odd thing happens in the middle of our passage. God, the master and great benefactor, switches roles. At the end of time, God "...will dress himself to serve..." and will have those good servants whom He found ready and waiting to recline back and He will wait on them (v. 37). It is a staggering reversal of roles that is not lost on a follower of Jesus during Advent. For Advent is about preparing for the awesome miracle of the incarnation (God in the flesh) becoming a reality. God has already stooped down so low as to be born a human. So it should come as no surprise to us that God will do this at the end. The only thing we must decide is if we are going to follow His example in the intermediate. Are we going to be found being both a benefactor and servant of others?

Prayer

Servant of all, who gives to each according to their need, help us to humbly care for those we come in contact with that we might fulfill the responsibility you have bestowed upon us, for your glory. Amen.

FRIDAY – DAY 6 – BE READY

Daily Psalm

> *As a father has compassion on his children,*
> *so the LORD has compassion on those who fear him;*
> *for he knows how we are formed,*
> *he remembers that we are dust.*
> *The life of mortals is like grass,*
> *they flourish like a flower of the field;*
> *the wind blows over it and it is gone,*
> *and its place remembers it no more.*
> *But from everlasting to everlasting*
> *the LORD's love is with those who fear him,*
> *and his righteousness with their children's children—*
> *with those who keep his covenant*
> *and remember to obey his precepts.*
> (Psalm 103:13-18)

Acts of Mercy

- Take a gift to a stranger who is in the hospital. (⊠)

- Babysit, shop, or run errands for someone you know is sick.

- Donate blood through the **American Red Cross**. (🎗) Visit http://www.redcross.org for more information.

Family Devotional

Read Matthew 24:15-31.

Have you ever missed an event because you got the time wrong? You put it on your calendar and carve out the time for it. You planned and prepared for it in advance. You got dressed and drove all the way there. Then there is the moment when you realize that something isn't right. The lights are off, there are no other cars in the parking

lot, and the doors are locked. You double-check the event details and let out a sigh of utter letdown as your eyes focus on the actual date and time. How could you have missed it?

Now, what do you think it was like preparing for Jesus' return in the early church? There were probably people who had heard Jesus teach and saw Him after His resurrection. Can you imagine their passion for following Jesus' teaching? Can you imagine their desire to tell others about who Jesus was and what He did? Can you imagine how they longed and prayed for Jesus' return? Now imagine if someone says they already saw Jesus return. How disappointing would that be?

It must have filled the original hearers of Matthew's gospel with great joy to hear that the return of the Son of Man would not be some small event. With people spreading lies of Jesus' return it would be good news to hear that it would be a worldwide event. Our passage describes the return of Jesus as lightning that is visible from east to west. In other words, the second Advent will be so dramatic that no one will be able to miss it.

We can participate in the intermediate Advent with the calm assurance that the second Advent cannot be missed. We can labor in faith as we witness to the good news that God comes to us, and rest in the hope that when He comes in glory it will be cosmic in scale.

Prayer

Jesus our Redeemer, who has ransomed humanity from death and destruction, we are grateful for the promise of your return and that you will be with us always even to the end of time. Amen.

SATURDAY – DAY 7 – BE READY

Daily Psalm

> *Why do the nations conspire*
> *and the peoples plot in vain?*
> *The kings of the earth rise up*
> *and the rulers band together*
> *against the LORD And against his anointed, saying,*
> *"Let us break their chains*
> *and throw off their shackles."*
> (Psalm 2:1-3)

Acts of Mercy

- Deliver goodies to and spend time with a shut-in.

- Visit someone you know in jail or reach out to someone who has been recently released from being incarcerated. Visit http://www.bgcprisonministries.com for more information.

- Sponsor **Angel Tree** children for Christmas. (🐑) Visit http://www.prisonfellowship.org/programs/angel-tree for more information.

Family Devotional

Read 2 Peter 3.

How do we respond when our acts of mercy are rejected? On several Christmases past, my wife and I found our attempts to spread care were unwanted. Once a homeless man turned up his nose at our offering of a granola bar and bottled water. An elderly shut-in criticized us for taking her to a Red Cross heating shelter when the ice had knocked out power for several days. A neighbor yelled from a second-story window that he wasn't coming to the door to accept our plate of Christmas cookies. Dumbfounded, confused, stunned, and

upset—a range of emotions we weren't expecting. When we try to care for others and their response is to complain or reject our care and concern for them, what should we do?

Our passage deals with the question of why the final Advent has not yet come. A new heaven and earth have been promised, but we still live in a sinful world that has not changed. The response is that God is patient, and is giving humanity time to repent and change their ways before the judgment comes. Our response should be to live holy lives while we await the new heaven and earth where righteousness is at home.

There is a parallel between Israel's waiting for the coming of God to be their shepherd and comforter and the Church's waiting for the return of Christ. In both cases, what is awaited is a world in which the goodness of God abounds. In the intermediate, we witness to God's goodness. By acts of mercy we show a world where righteousness is not at home, that unmerited love is God's way, and the ultimate way the new heaven and new earth will be like.

Prayer

Righteous One, who judges with loving kindness, help us to respond with patience and grace when our attempts to share your mercy are rejected, that we may be faithful to your call to love in this fallen world. Amen.

SUNDAY – DAY 8

Reflection on Matthew 3:1-12

Produce fruit in keeping with repentance. (Matthew 3:8)

Do as I Say, Not as I Do

The "do as I say, not as I do" phrase is often repeated by parents attempting to instruct their children. The children quickly pick up on the discontinuity between their parents' speech and actions. In most cases, it is not an issue. But there are those crucial moments in life that parents need to model their instruction for their children.

In the not-so-distant past a father recorded a disciplinary video where he rebuked his teenage daughter for her degrading posts on a social network regarding her parents. The video included a rant by the father and ended with him shooting her laptop. He proceeded to post the video on social media sites.

Clearly the father was implicitly communicating, "Do as I say, not as I do." He denounced her for posting degrading remarks and causing her parents public shame. While at the same time that is exactly what he did. His message degraded his daughter and caused her public shame. This is one of those crucial moments in life where a parent's message should have been demonstrated by their actions.

John's Message and Life

John the Baptist is a perfect example of one whose life matched his message. John announced, "Repent, for the kingdom of heaven has come near." John delivered the message in the desert away from the villages and cities. John's location symbolizes the coming of a new exodus and it reflected a renouncement of the current culture, which is just one of the prices a true prophet of God pays. Second, John wore camel hair clothing which resembled the typical dress of the poor. Finally, John ate locusts and wild honey which was a diet found among the poorest of the poor. John's location, clothing, and diet open up the question for us, *Have we really given up everything?*

When John's announcement and life are heard and observed together, we clearly understand that repentance is life-changing. Repentance is a returning to God, not merely a change of mind. It means that we will have to give up everything, including some of the most basic elements of life—like where we live, what we wear, and what we eat.

However, the focus is not so much about being like John the Baptist but recognizing ourselves as the Pharisees and Sadducees. We are called to respond to John's message of the coming kingdom. We're asked to become disciples and to be fruitful. The image of a tree bearing fruit demands that a professedly repentant person's life match one's profession. Is an apple tree that doesn't produce apples really an apple tree? In short, what we do and what we say must be in harmony.

Yet Matthew also expects his community, as well as us today, to recognize that we are susceptible to becoming like these Pharisees (Matthew 24:48-51; Amos 5:18-20). The Christian equivalent of "We have Abraham as our Father" is "We have Christ as our Savior." The temptation of many Christians who have been born again is to rest on this pharisaical idea. We can believe that since we had an experience of coming to know Christ as Savior means that we need not bear the fruit of that reality of Christ in our life. The error that we often make is assuming that faith in Christ merely means mental acceptance. However, we are not merely to possess faith but practice faithfulness each day, following the Messiah's way of life.

Be Fruitful

If we are to take John the Baptist's message seriously we must, unlike the Pharisees, be willing to change all of our preconceptions about who we think the Messiah should be. We must be open to allowing God to show us a new and deeper understanding of who He is. And above all, we must be willing to follow Christ, wherever He leads us.

Following Christ will lead us to bear a particular kind of fruit. We will produce the fruit of the kingdom. And that fruit will be the justice, righteousness, and care for the poor that Isaiah tells us God's Chosen One will be about. We will engage in acts of mercy for Christ

is merciful. We will celebrate His presence by being present with the lonely. We will keep in step with the Spirit and hope that we might be found at His return doing as He said and did.

Acts of Piety

- Write a poem or song about what the Lord is showing you through the acts of mercy.

- Share thoughts, photos, or video of your acts of mercy this week with a friend or through a blog.

- Pray for strength, patience, energy, and blessings for those who are daily God's hands and feet.

MONDAY – DAY 9 – BE FRUITFUL

Daily Psalm

At midnight I rise to give you thanks
for your righteous laws.
I am a friend to all who fear you,
to all who follow your precepts.
The earth is filled with your love, LORD;
teach me your decrees.
(Psalm 119:62-64)

Acts of Mercy

- Mail a grocery or restaurant gift card to someone. (✉)

- Share baked goods or fresh fruit with coworkers, classmates, or neighbors.

- Volunteer at a local soup kitchen or food bank. (🐾)

Family Devotional

Read John 15:1-12.

The Advent season is a time to focus on relationships. You work hard to cut out time for family gatherings. You make time to see old friends who are in town for the holidays. Or, you travel long distances to visit extended family. You expect the season to be a time to reconnect with people.

Reconnecting with loved ones who live out of town can be difficult. The physical space between you means you've missed out on being together during the routines of life. The limited amount of time you get to spend with them lends itself well to focusing on big event stories, but you miss out on the daily stories of joys and pains. In short, your connection with out-of-town friends and family becomes an exercise in getting familiar with one another all the while the deep connection becomes allusive.

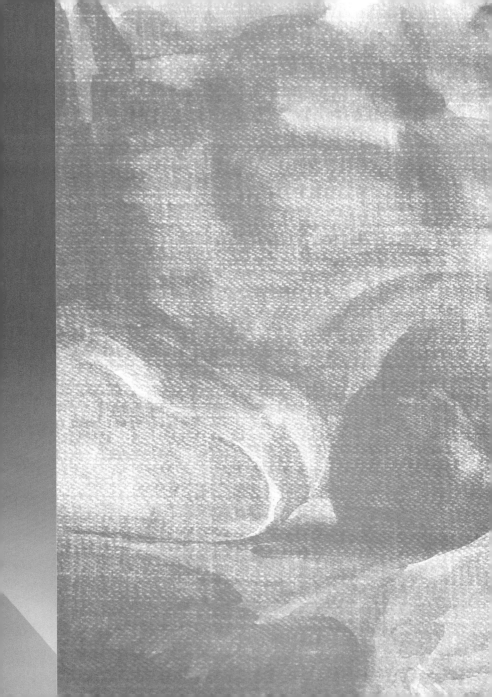

In our passage today, Jesus teaches His disciples the nature of their relationship. They are supposed to be like a fruit-bearing vine. Receiving and giving back in an inseparable, life-giving, deep, and natural relationship with one another produces fruit in the life of the disciple. Jesus goes on to say that His disciple is to remain in Him and He will remain in them. The word "remain," in some translations "abide," is a meaningful word in the gospel of John. In John, abiding is a description of Jesus' relationship with the Father. It is their relationship of abiding in one another that gives Jesus the confidence to say that those who have seen Him have seen the Father. The abiding characteristic of the Father and Son's dynamic relationship is now extended to the disciples and Jesus. In a real way, as we abide in Christ He is made known to others through us.

In the intermediate, our relationship with Jesus is well beyond familiar. Our abiding relationship with Jesus is nurtured by our continued obedience to His way of life. Jesus says it is by obeying His teachings that we reflect the abiding relationship of the Father and the Son. And loving one another is central to Jesus' way of life for us. As believers in mutual self-surrender to one another, the fruit of love begins to emerge in the body of Christ. And that fruit pours out into our neighborhoods and community as acts of mercy. This is how we are to celebrate Advent: By revealing Christ's abiding presence as the Church through bearing the fruit of our mutual Christ-like love for one another. This is the meaning of waiting for His coming and being found ready.

Prayer

Comforter, who comes to your faithful to give strength, we ask that you would comfort all those who are sick and lonely through your chosen people. Amen.

TUESDAY – DAY 10 – BE FRUITFUL

Daily Psalm

> But whose delight is in the law of the LORD,
>   and who meditates on his law day and night.
> That person is like a tree planted by streams of water,
>   which yields its fruit in season
> and whose leaf does not wither—
>   whatever they do prospers.
> Not so the wicked!
>   They are like chaff
>   that the wind blows away.
>   (Psalm 1:2-4)

Acts of Mercy

- Pack or purchase an extra drink for lunch to give to a classmate or coworker. (✉)

- Start an online fundraising campaign for, or donate to, **Charity:Water**. (★) Visit https://www.charitywater.org/ for more information.

- Set up a free hot cocoa/lemonade stand. (❧ , ✉)

Family Devotional

Read Colossians 1:3-14.

In the United Methodist Church there is a tradition of those desiring to become pastors being asked the question, *Have you fruit?* I suggest that this simple question is not just for those wishing to be clergy. This is a question for all of us and our churches, *Is there any fruit in my life?* The question should be asked frequently and honestly by each believer and by faith communities.

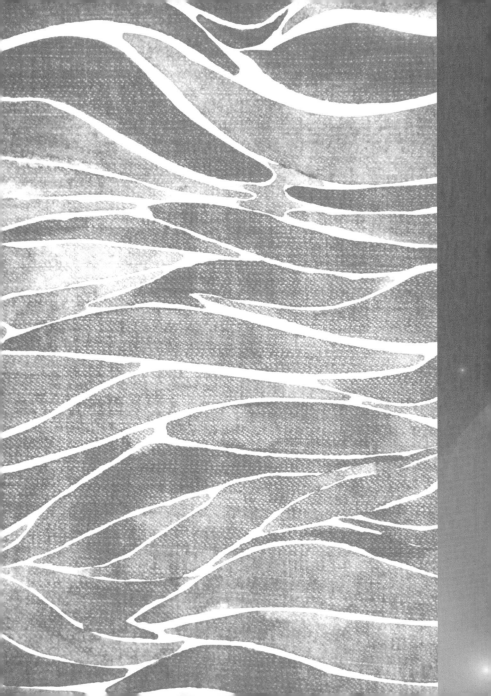

The Advent is like the Christian version of the NFL playoffs. Most churches treat it as a time to prepare for the "big game" which is either their Christmas Eve or Christmas Sunday service. No matter how your church celebrates Christmas, it tends to be one of two seasons—the other being Easter—when churches stack program on top of program. But in all of the activity, I wonder how many of us have stopped to ask the simple question, *Is there any fruit?* I'm not bashing activity during the Advent season. I just wonder how much of it is motivated by the expectation that it will bear the fruit of the gospel or if it will merely be entertainment for the church.

The church in Colossae was praised for their fruitfulness. The apostle Paul praised them because he heard of their faith in Jesus, their love for all God's people, and the hope they have from receiving the gospel. It is the gospel that is bearing fruit among them that Paul is so excited about. One of the fruits that it is producing is a mutual self-surrendering love in the Spirit (v. 8). As we know from yesterday, this type of love reveals Christ's abiding presence in the life of the church.

We all have images and stories of fruitless churches and believers. The story of the church that closes its doors with no one in the community noticing can be told in numerous variations. Stories of the believer who warms the pew but never seems to have the time or energy to reach out to a next-door neighbor are all too common. But the point of Advent is not despair in the darkness but to hope in the light.

So here is the first question, *Is there any fruit in your church?* This is an honest question that you should ask your small group and/or church family. You should discern together if the activities of your church are merely clanging symbols, or if they are the expressions of your love in the Spirit.

Here is the second question, which is similar to the first, *Is there any fruit in your life?* This question should be asked with other believers. Oftentimes we can be our own worst critic and so we would do well to discern the answer to this question with a fellow believer.

Once again, Advent is a season of hope. And these types of questions should lead us to the hope that is ours in Christ Jesus. If you find yourself despairing over these questions, the apostle Paul's prayer is appropriate, "We continually ask God to fill you with the knowledge of his will through all the wisdom and understanding that the Spirit gives, so that you may live a life worthy of the Lord and please him in every way: bearing fruit in every good work" (vv. 9-10).

Prayer

True Vine, who gives life and brings forth fruit at the appointed time, open us up to a life of deep intimacy with you that sustains us through the longest spiritual droughts. We ask this for your glory. Amen.

WEDNESDAY – DAY 11 – BE FRUITFUL

Daily Psalm

> I will listen to what God the LORD says;
> > he promises peace to his people, his faithful servants—
> > but let them not turn to folly.
> Surely his salvation is near those who fear him,
> > that his glory may dwell in our land.
> Love and faithfulness meet together;
> > righteousness and peace kiss each other.
> Faithfulness springs forth from the earth,
> > and righteousness looks down from heaven.
> The LORD will indeed give what is good,
> > and our land will yield its harvest.
> Righteousness goes before him
> > and prepares the way for his steps.
> > > (Psalm 85:8-13)

Acts of Mercy

- Hold the door open for someone every time you enter/leave a public place.

- Invite someone new to sit at your lunch table or invite a new family to your house.

- Package shoeboxes (❧) for **Samaritan's Purse's Operation Christmas Child** (★). Visit http://www.samaritanspurse.org/index.php/occ/ for more information.

Family Devotional

Read 2 Peter 1:3-11.

There I was standing in line for my flight to a conference for work. I was glad I made it to the gate on time even though I cut it close. All of a sudden I was hit by the feeling that I had forgotten something. Was it my work folder? No. Was it my cell phone charger? No. My hands began patting around my coat. Then it hit me, I didn't have my wallet. My mind jumped into hyper-drive trying to remember the last place I had it. I remembered that I took it out of my pocket when I got into the car. So I hurried to my car in hopes that the plane would somehow encounter some kind of delay to give me enough time to get what I needed in order to leave for the trip.

The feeling of not having everything you need for a trip can create anxiety. The excitement of preparing for a trip can be ripped away in the moment of realizing that you can't go because you didn't have one of the most essential things.

It is a great comfort that Peter begins this passage with the calm reassurance that we have everything we need to live a godly life. It is by God's own glory and goodness that we are provided the resources we need to take the journey of the Christian life. This means that we don't need to rely on our own abilities to grow and produce fruit. In other words, the power to grow doesn't come from us. It is God the Spirit living inside us that is the source and power of our growth.

All our growth as Christ-followers begins with faith. But faith is not the end for us. It is merely the starting point of the virtues that grow in the life of a believer. The goal of our growth is love. It is the pinnacle virtue in the list Peter highlights in verses 5-7. Author Richard Bauckham says this concerning the list of virtues:

> Christian love is the crowning virtue to which all the others must contribute. In a list of this kind, the last item has unique significance. It is not just the most important virtue, but also the virtue which encompasses all the others. Love is the overriding ethical principle from which the other virtues gain their meaning and validity.[6]

As we celebrate Advent by practicing acts of mercy, we need not worry if we are loving enough. Rather we are invited to trust that God has supplied us everything we need. So we are free to faithfully follow Jesus' example of loving the least, being assured that God will produce the fruit.

Prayer

Bread of Life, who nourishes your people with the eternal food, may we be found giving life to those who are in the greatest need when you return. Amen.

THURSDAY – DAY 12 – BE FRUITFUL

Daily Psalm

> *Righteousness and justice are the foundation of your throne;*
>> *love and faithfulness go before you.*
> *Blessed are those who have learned to acclaim you,*
>> *who walk in the light of your presence, LORD.*
> *They rejoice in your name all day long;*
>> *they celebrate your righteousness.*
>> (Psalm 89:14-16)

Acts of Mercy

- Put together a care package for a homeless person or family in need. (✉)

- Sort through your closets to donate clothing to a thrift store.

- Pass out gloves, hats, and scarves outside a sledding spot or skating rink. (🐾, ✉)

Family Devotional

Read Ephesians 5:1-2.

Louis Albert Banks tells a story about a man who was spending a summer near the shores of Lake Superior. One day he came upon an old pine that had been blown down by a recent storm. Knowing something about trees, he was intrigued by the huge evergreen lying on the ground. He examined it closely and figured it was at least 250 years old. What impressed him most, however, was what he discovered when he stripped away the bark. It was evident to him that on the day the tree fell it was still growing.[7]

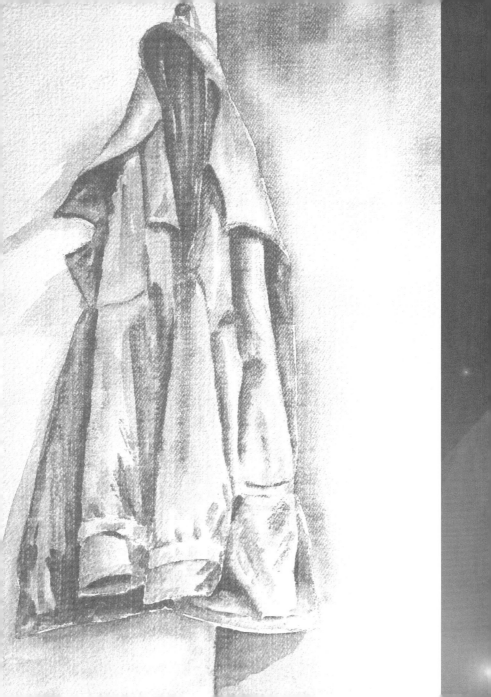

That's the way it should be in the life of the believer. The years pass and our physical strength declines. The outward person perishes but the inner person should keep on developing—mentally, emotionally, and above all spiritually—until the day we die. In fact, the Word of God is quite clear on the subject of growth. God wants His followers to grow and expects them to grow right up until the very end of the age.

When we consider growing into the likeness of God, there are some things that are off limits: We can't become all-knowing, all-powerful, and ever-present. The overlap between us and our creator has limits. That being said, there is still considerable room for growth.

Here are six traits we might consider worth imitating in our pursuit of bearing the image of Christ to our world. First, God expressly calls us to emulate the *holiness* that is on display as God acts mercifully, justly, rightly, and with no hint of darkness among us throughout history. Second, God's *goodness* revealed in His acts to put others' interests before His own is an attribute we can develop and demonstrate. Third, to act from a place motivated by *love* (rather than out of obligation or fear) is what sets Jesus apart. I believe it should set His followers apart as well. Fourth, God has a perfect track record of keeping promises and providing for His people. He is dependable, and our challenge is to reflect that integrity and *trustworthiness*. Fifth, from walking in the cool of the afternoon, to a cloud in front of Israel, to a baby lying in a manger, God will always be *present*. We can emulate this trait by growing in our awareness, alertness, and attentiveness to be present in each moment. Sixth, God is on the move and at work. God is *missional*—creating, relating, reforming, and restoring. Our mandate is to stop working on our thing and be about noticing and joining God at work in our midst.

As we participate in Advent this year, it will be good to keep in mind these traits of God and this high calling to be imitators. It is the hope that this season will be another one of growth as you celebrate the reality that our God has come to rescue, is coming to comfort, and will be coming again in glory.

Prayer

Almighty Refiner, who purifies your people like pure gold, grant that we might be so filled with your Spirit that our every thought, word and deed would be imitations of your holy presence in our life. Amen.

FRIDAY – DAY 13 – BE FRUITFUL

Daily Psalm

> They celebrate your abundant goodness
> and joyfully sing of your righteousness.
> The LORD is gracious and compassionate,
> slow to anger and rich in love.
> The LORD is good to all;
> he has compassion on all he has made.
> All your works praise you, LORD;
> your faithful people extol you.
> (Psalm 145:7-10)

Acts of Mercy

- Sign up to be an organ donor. Visit http://www.organdonor.gov/ for more information.

- Visit someone you know in the hospital or do something for him/her (wash and fill up his/her car, hire a house-cleaning service, restock their kitchen with groceries, and so on).

- Skip a movie, concert, or sporting event and use the money ($) saved to support **Doctors Without Borders** (★). Visit http://www.doctorswithoutborders.org/ for more information.

Family Devotional

Read James 3:13-18.

We live in a world where ambition is required. If you aren't ambitious, you are a slacker. If "money makes the world go around," ambition is the engine that turns it. Some kinds of ambition are good, but the problem with most of our ambitions is that they are all about us. And when our ambitions are essentially selfish, we tend to adopt an "any means to the end" approach. I think we can agree that when selfish interest dominates our ambitions, our principles are the first to go.

James was very concerned about this tendency. That's why he wrote to warn Christians about the effects of selfish ambition on people and on the communities to which they belonged. He says, "For where you have envy and selfish ambition, there you find disorder and every evil practice" (v. 16). I'm not sure anyone could have said it better. The alternative, from James' perspective, is "the wisdom that comes from above." For James, the real goal of the one who seeks the meaning of life is *wisdom*. Wisdom that is a way of life defined by walking in God's ways—humility, meekness, gentleness, integrity, peace, and mercy! For James, wisdom is about making our faith real.

That's not really what we look for in life. We see the meaning of life in terms of what we can achieve (success), who knows our name (fame), and what we have acquired (wealth). And we see the meaning of life in terms of what it takes to get there. Selfish ambition, and often envy, drives us.

We see these two types of wisdom on display during the Advent season. There are those who choose to rush through Advent with selfish ambition. They will trample others down to grab the last toy from the shelf because their kid is more important. They'll cut people off to get ahead in traffic on the way to work because their job is more important. They'll yell at the waitresses and cashiers who don't work quickly enough because their time is more important. Then there are those who will take the path of "the wisdom that comes from above." They will engage in the pure actions of being considerate. They will be full of mercy for the weak and produce the fruit of love in their actions. They will engage in sincere conversations as they practice being present with the people around them. As you seek to participate in Advent, may you bear the fruit of the wisdom from above.

Prayer

Author of Peace, who writes the law of love onto our hearts, announce in our actions and speech the good news of the Prince of Peace leading to the fruit of the gospel among all people. We ask in the name of one who is to come, Jesus Christ. Amen.

SATURDAY – DAY 14 – BE FRUITFUL

Daily Psalm

> Direct me in the path of your commands,
>> for there I find delight.
>
> Turn my heart toward your statutes
>> and not toward selfish gain.
>
> Turn my eyes away from worthless things;
>> preserve my life according to your word.
>
> (Psalm 119:35-37)

Acts of Mercy

- Send an encouragement card to someone battling addiction.

- Sign up to disciple a prisoner. Visit http://www.prisonfellowship.org/get-involved/in-prison/ for more information.

- Volunteer at an area Department of Corrections or Juvenile Detention Center. (🎥)

Family Devotional

Read Galatians 5:16-25.

In high school, I worked part-time at a department store. I drew the short straw and had to work the dreaded Black Friday opening shift. This particular year was the Furby® craze and I had to be a part of the team that handed them out. I don't know whose idea it was, but they chose to put these toys in a safe in the sporting goods department. The procedure was first-come-first-serve. When a customer would arrive and ask for one of these toys, we instructed this person to take a number and go to the back of the line. When his or her number was called, this person was allowed to come forward and pick up one or two.

Everything was going smoothly until one person got a little greedy. A woman stepped up and picked two. However, she then waited at the front and bartered with the first person who only chose one in order to get this person's second toy, which she offered to buy. A guy about halfway back in line saw that this lady had three Furbies®, rather than the allotted one or two. In a fit of rage, he started screaming at her to put one back. The lady shouted back a few choice words of her own. In response, the guy picked up a softball and threw it at her head. Crazy, right?

We all probably wish this was an uncommon story. But we know all too well that the preparations for Christmas bring out the best and worst in people. We get to see the dark side of human indignity and the beauty of the human flourishing during this time of the year.

In the intermediate we experience two modes of existence in the world all the time. These two modes are a result of the life, death, and resurrection of Jesus—the Son of God. The one mode is characterized by human indignity. Our passage calls it "the flesh" and says that it is seen in the acts which are selfish ambition, dissensions, factions, and envy. The other mode is characterized by human flourishing. Our passage calls it "the Spirit" and says that it is manifested in the fruit of the Spirit which are love, joy, peace, forbearance, kindness, goodness, faithfulness, gentleness, and self-control.

The question for us this Advent is, *Which mode do you operate in?* For those who have confessed Jesus as Lord, the Scriptures say that the desires of the flesh have been crucified and that you have been made alive in the Spirit. If we get out of step with the Spirit then we can return to operating in the mode of the flesh. Are you keeping in step with the Spirit this Advent season? Are you preparing for the return of the Lord by loving God and neighbor? Are you deeply concerned with the least and serving them with your whole heart?

Prayer

Holy One, who condescended to your creation, may your Holy Spirit be a sole guide so that we might operate in the Spirit and cast out the way of this present world order from our hearts and minds. For your honor we pray. Amen.

SUNDAY – DAY 15

Reflection on Matthew 11:2-11

Blessed is anyone who takes no offense at me. (Matthew 11:6, NRSV)

Expectations

Advent is a time of expectation. In preparing for Christmas, we set expectations for our time with family and friends. Children write out their lists with expectations of gifts they'll receive. Parents purchase and wrap presents with expectations of their children's reactions when they open them. We set expectations for our vacation time. Some plan on getting long lists of household chores crossed off, others intend to stay in sweats all day watching television with the family, some plan on getting ahead on work projects, and others anticipate spending all their time hanging out with friends. Consciously or not, our expectations impact our day-to-day decisions.

As we wait for the return of Christ, expectations for who Christ is, what life is all about, and who we are come to the surface. These expectations are nothing new, as people waited for the first Advent of the Messiah, they set expectations, too. What type of kingdom were they expecting? What kind of messiah were they looking, praying, and hoping for? During that first Advent, several Jewish groups emerged, each with unique expectations. The Sadducees, Zealots, Pharisees, and Essenes all believed that God's kingdom would mean establishing God's perfect rule in the world. But what is more insightful to their expectations is how they prepared for it. They all lived their lives in a particular way, believing that what they did was linked to how God's kingdom and the messiah would be.

The first group were the Sadducees. The Sadducees were the priests in the temple during this period because they compromised with Herod and the Roman Empire regarding Jewish law and traditions. This provided them with comfortable lives and political popularity. Their preparations reveal that they expected the messiah to establish a political kingdom, but for now they were content to work with the empire and worship in the temple.

The Zealots were completely opposite from the Sadducees. They believed the messiah and the kingdom would come by way of military revolt. So they gave their life to the cause of freedom fighting against the Roman Empire. Their preparations reveal expectations that the messiah would be a military leader and that God's kingdom would come with force and free the Jewish people from oppression.

The Pharisees were fanatics of the Law (Torah). They lived their life in absolute obedience to the Law and drove all Jewish people to do the same. They even added laws just to make sure that they didn't come close to being disobedient. Their preparations reveal expectations that the messiah would be a great teacher of the Law and the kingdom of God would mean God ruled perfectly and with complete obedience from His people.

Finally, the Essenes were a group that withdrew from the contemporary culture and life of their day. They created monastic communities in the desert believing that through strict adherence to prayer and fasting they could speed up the day when the messiah and kingdom would be established. Their lives reveal expectations that the kingdom of God would be nothing like this world, but a spiritual reality.

Should We Expect Someone Else?

John the Baptist had given his life in preparation for the Messiah and kingdom to come. John already believed that Jesus was the Messiah. But in our passage today he is thrown into prison and it seems as though he is becoming anxious and possibly doubting what he knows about Jesus. So he sends a couple of his disciples to ask Jesus the same question all the Jewish groups want to know, "Should we expect someone else?"

Jesus replies, "Go and tell John what you hear and see: the blind receive their sight, the lame walk, the lepers are cleansed, the deaf hear, the dead are raised, and the poor have good news brought to them. And blessed is anyone who takes no offense at me" (Matthew 11:4-6, NRSV)

Jesus is the Messiah. He forgives sins and calls people to follow Him as He follows God. And along the way, He demonstrates that God's redeeming and restoring power is at work through Him. If we have eyes to see and ears to hear, we realize that it is Jesus who is the kingdom. It is through Jesus that we come to know God's beautiful rule in our lives. It is by following Jesus that we see God's redeeming and restoring power explode into our world.

As you can imagine, the various Jewish groups may not be so happy with this answer. To the Zealot who is expecting military might and political freedom, Jesus is offensive. To the Sadducee content with how things are, Jesus is offensive. To the Pharisee that desires religious purity and obedience to God, Jesus is offensive. To the Essene who wants nothing to do with the current state of this world, Jesus is offensive. Jesus doesn't fulfill their expectations for God's Messiah and kingdom.

Be Blessed

Expectations haven't changed much in 2,000 years. The way that the four Jewish groups prepared for the first Advent is a lot like how many of us prepare for the second. The contemporary Zealots are aggressively ready to battle for truth and goodness with Jesus. They put the reason for the season in everyone's face and demand that every cashier tell them "Merry Christmas." The contemporary Sadducees are the accommodators. They are passionate about the religion of Christianity but tend to tame Jesus in order to be relevant. They serve others because it's trendy and talk about Jesus as though He is their pal. What happens is that Jesus ends up being everyone's buddy and nobody's Lord. The contemporary Pharisee operates out of a certainty of belief rather than confidence in Jesus. They see the world in religiously black and white terms and they police the church for anyone who doesn't have the same zeal they have for keeping the Word of God. The contemporary Essenes see this world as a distraction from a real relationship with God. They are so heavenly minded that they are no earthly good to anyone. They are more concerned about self-preservation then following Jesus in word and deed.

So Jesus' answer to John is for us today. Do we take offense at Jesus? Does He not meet our expectations? Are we preparing for a different messiah than God's Messiah? The truth is that if we really embrace Jesus' words and actions and reach to the least and lonely we may be offended. We may find ourselves with the wrong kind of people. We may find ourselves among folks who need to know the good news of the God who comes. Are you willing to risk it this Advent season? Are you willing to celebrate by acting mercifully like Jesus? Are you willing to be blessed by surrendering your expectations and embracing Jesus' way of life?

Acts of Piety

- Draw a picture or make a collage representing someone you encountered through acts of mercy.

- Speak to someone who doesn't know Jesus personally and tell them how He has changed your life.

- Pray that God will teach you more about His love as you continue sharing it with others.

MONDAY – DAY 16 – BE BLESSED

Daily Psalm

> Good and upright is the LORD;
> > therefore he instructs sinners in his ways.
> He guides the humble in what is right
> > and teaches them his way.
> All the ways of the LORD are loving and faithful
> > toward those who keep the demands of his covenant.
> For the sake of your name, LORD,
> > forgive my iniquity, though it is great.
> > > (Psalm 25:8-11)

Acts of Mercy

- Tape quarters to a snack or soda vending machine. (✉)

- Skip the restaurant and dine on leftovers, use the money saved ($) to support **Feeding America** (★). Visit http://feedingamerica.org/ for more information.

- Volunteer to be a bell ringer for the Red Kettle Campaign (🔔) through the **Salvation Army** (★). Visit http://www.salvationarmyusa.org for more information.

Family Devotional

Read Matthew 9:9-13.

In 1st century Jewish customs the meal was a sign of fellowship, love, and acceptance. The meal was a way to tell someone that they were accepted and were part of your group. Meal-sharing was done by kings when a covenant was made. It was also done when a "stranger" became a part of a community. So Levi's meal was a way for him to say to Jesus, "I accept you and I want to be a part of your group." It was also a way for Jesus to tell Levi, the tax collectors, and sinners that gathered they were accepted and loved by God too.

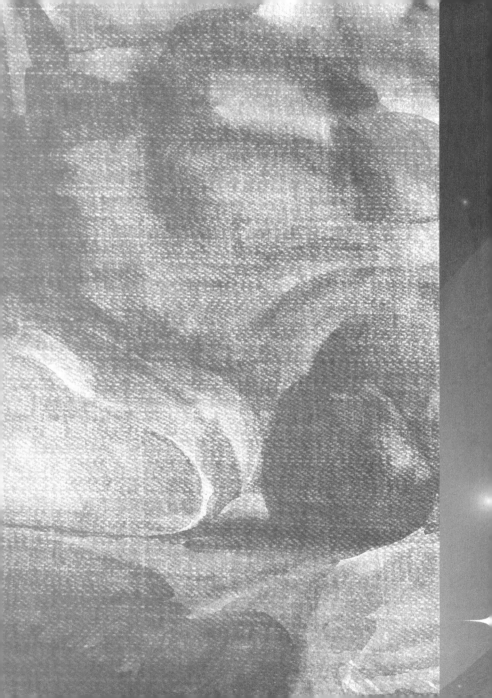

But who are these other people with whom Jesus is eating? *Hamartolos,* the Greek word translated "sinners," comes from *hamartia* which is translated "sin" throughout the New Testament. *Hamartia* has different meanings in various passages. Paul uses it to mean missing the mark; John uses it as disobeying a divine law; Luke uses it as an evil deed. From our location as readers of this passage it seems harsh for people like the Pharisees to enter a place and immediately label people with the term "sinners." Whoever these people are, it seems clear that Jesus does not have the same view as the Pharisees.

The Pharisees ask the disciples, "Why does your teacher eat with tax collectors and sinners?" Jesus uses the Pharisees' question to reveal His mission: To show the world that God "desires mercy, not sacrifice" (Hosea 6:6) from His people and that He has come to call sinners to repentance. Jesus has been called to those who are the outcasts in order that they too may know the mercy of God.

As we celebrate Advent this year, we work to show through daily acts of mercy the love of God in our world. Have you been playing it too safe? Have you focused most of your activity on those who really need it? If we are seeking to follow Jesus in these daily acts, we must be willing to go to the people who are unnoticed, overlooked, and often cast out of the presence of "good Christians." We must be willing to invite the sinner to a meal and let them know that they are welcomed home by the God who comes.

Prayer

God of mercy, who came to call sinners home, we ask that you give us the compassion to pour your love onto the broken and weak through the power of your Spirit. Amen.

TUESDAY – DAY 17 – BE BLESSED

Daily Psalm

> You answer us with awesome and righteous deeds,
>   God our Savior,
> the hope of all the ends of the earth
>   and of the farthest seas,
> who formed the mountains by your power,
>   having armed yourself with strength,
> who stilled the roaring of the seas,
>   the roaring of their waves,
>   and the turmoil of the nations.
> The whole earth is filled with awe at your wonders;
>   where morning dawns, where evening fades,
>   you call forth songs of joy.
>   (Psalm 65:5-8)

Acts of Mercy

- Pay for someone's coffee. (✉)

- Find out the favorite drink of someone special or meaningful in your life (parent, teacher, coworker) and get it for him/her.

- If you normally exchange small gifts with classmates/coworkers for Christmas, make a donation ($) in their name for **Blood: Water Mission** (★) and request they do so for you in lieu of a gift. Visit http://www.bloodwatermission.org/ for more information.

Family Devotional

Read Matthew 9:1-8.

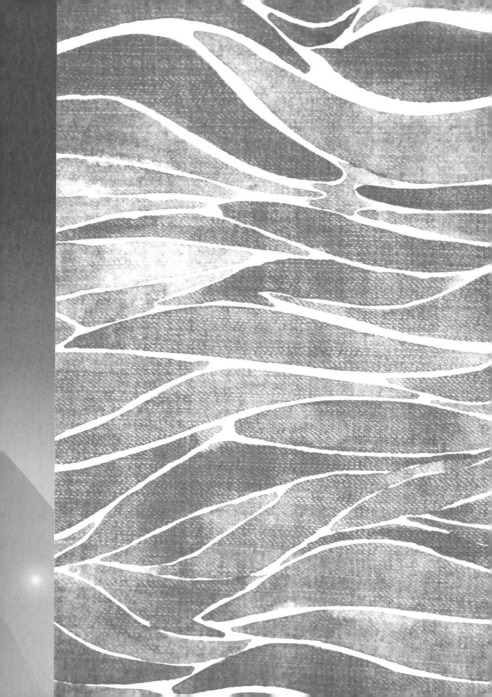

Are you still amazed at Jesus' power to transform a life? Oftentimes we get years away from experiencing God's transformational power and begin to wonder if Jesus Christ can still change people's lives. Maybe you became a Christian when you were a teen and you're now in your fifties and can't remember another time you've experienced dramatic life transformation. Or perhaps your church hasn't seen someone surrender their life to Christ in several years. You may begin to read a passage like today's and dismiss how much faith it takes to come to Jesus with the expectation that He will transform.

The passage begins with Jesus in His hometown. A paralyzed man is brought to Jesus by the man's friends. The faith that it takes for this group of friends to believe that this Jesus whom they have heard about can heal their friend is immense. They are probably trusting in the word of other friends who have heard and seen Jesus. They care deeply for their friend and are desperate for him to be given new life. So they carry their friend to Jesus. Jesus saw their faith and told the paralyzed man his sins were forgiven.

Wait. What? They want their friend healed and Jesus forgives his sins? That's not the type of transformation that they were looking for. That wasn't what they wanted from Jesus. Ironically, the religious leaders didn't like that Jesus forgave the man's sins. They said to each other, "blasphemer." It is as though Jesus was trying to undercut everyone's expectations in this story. Or maybe Jesus was trying to raise all of their expectations.

This Advent season might be a time when Christ is trying to raise our expectations once again. You are in a position to be filled with awe as you boldly act mercifully and pray that God will intervene in the lives of the weak. You are ready if you are daring to bring your friends the good news that they can come back to God and follow Christ with you. As we move closer to the celebration of the first Advent, let us keep in mind that the miracle of God coming to us is not a "back then" reality but a present and living hope.

Prayer

Mighty God, who can transform hearts of stone, fill us with your Spirit so that we may be inspired to humbly connect with people today and passionately share your mercy for your glory and honor. Amen.

WEDNESDAY – DAY 18 – BE BLESSED

Daily Psalm

> *The LORD is close to the brokenhearted*
> *and saves those who are crushed in spirit.*
> *The righteous person may have many troubles,*
> *but the LORD delivers him from them all;*
> *he protects all his bones,*
> *not one of them will be broken.*
> *Evil will slay the wicked;*
> *the foes of the righteous will be condemned.*
> *The LORD will rescue his servants;*
> *no one who takes refuge in him will be condemned.*
> (Psalm 34:18-22)

Acts of Mercy

- Invite someone who may be alone during the holidays into your home.

- Invite someone to come to church with you.

- Cancel or downgrade a luxury utility in your home (such as cable, data plan, newspaper delivery, and so on) to sponsor a child ($) through **Compassion International** (★). Visit http://www.compassion.com/ for more information.

Family Devotional

Read Matthew 8:1-4.

In our passage today, Jesus had large crowds following Him. This leads us to believe that the man approaching Jesus knows of His ministry and ability to perform miracles. The man comes begging on his knees to be healed. The man comes for self-centered reasons, which seems to be why everyone comes to Jesus. We are all broken emotionally, socially, spiritually, physically, and economically and we

want Jesus to "heal us." In other words, all who "come to Jesus" recognize their need and by the Spirit see that their need is ultimately fulfilled in Him.

This is one of the great gifts of the Advent season. It is a time for the whole church to recognize our mutual need of Christ. We can do nothing to hurry up the process of Christ's return or make God's work of redeeming and restoring the world complete. We must recognize that we live in dependence upon Christ to use us as His hands and feet in the world today.

Jesus graciously touches the man and his leprosy. Leprosy was a disease that made a person an outcast from society. Jesus' touch was probably the first touch the man had felt in a long time. His touch would have reconnected the man to another human being while at the same time sacrificing His own ability to participate in worship, for now He would be unclean. For Jesus to simply have given the man the experience of human contact would have been a beautiful act of love.

As we are going out each day to do acts of mercy, Jesus' action in this passage challenges us to go outside our religious comfort zone. It pushes us to go to the people who are outcast from our churches. It begs the question, *Will you risk your ability to participate in worship in order show love to the unwanted?*

After Jesus heals the man, He asks him to fulfill the sacrifice required by the covenant. Jesus does not wait to see if the man is going to be obedient to Him before He gives him what he seeks. Have you seen this in the church? We often put requirements on loving and caring for others in need. They have to come to a Sunday service before we give them assistance. They have to clean up before we shake their hand or give them a hug. They must straighten up their lives before they can worship among us. This is a season where we recognize our dependence on Christ, we risk it all in order to love and we resist putting requirements on the needy in order to love them. This is how we are invited to celebrate the coming of our Lord.

Prayer

God of loving kindness, whose faithfulness knows no end, may your patience with us endure as we wake up to the reality that we are your hands that should extend to the whole world through the energizing presence of your Son we pray. Amen.

THURSDAY – DAY 19 – BE BLESSED

Daily Psalm

> For the LORD is the great God,
> the great King above all gods.
> In his hand are the depths of the earth,
> and the mountain peaks belong to him.
> The sea is his, for he made it,
> and his hands formed the dry land.
> Come, let us bow down in worship,
> let us kneel before the LORD our Maker;
> for he is our God
> and we are the people of his pasture,
> the flock under his care.
> (Psalm 95:3-7)

Acts of Mercy

- Purchase a gift card at a clothing store and hand it to another customer as you leave. (✉)

- Leave laundry detergent and dryer sheets or load quarters at the laundromat. (✉)

- Purchase new or donate extra coats to those who need them via **OneWarmCoat.** (🧤) Visit http://onewarmcoat.org/ for more information.

Family Devotional

Read John 8.

Acting mercifully in our world is not easy. It requires that we are willing to enter difficult and challenging situations with hope. Mass media overwhelms us with stories of hunger, homelessness, poverty, war, and destruction. We are rarely exposed to stories of goodness, healing, abundant provision, and peace. So we can often feel like being hopeful in our world is pointless.

In our passage today, Jesus could have adopted a hopeless posture. When the woman is brought to Him by the scribes and Pharisees He could have been overwhelmed by the evil in their hearts and action. He could have given into their unrelenting desire to oppose Him and simply responded "I don't care." Instead Jesus bent down.

Jesus speaks to the woman from a "bent down" position. He looks up only to question the hearts of the accusers. Then, He bends back down and writes in the dirt as He engages the woman in a conversation.

"Woman where are they, has no one condemned you?" Jesus asks.

"No one, Lord," she said.

"Then neither do I condemn you," Jesus declared. "Go now and leave your life of sin."

In this brief exchange, Jesus overcomes the evil intent of the scribes and Pharisees by exposing their hearts. And then with no regard for religious etiquette, He has a conversation with a woman who had been caught in adultery. The end result is a healing that gives dignity back to the woman.

Michael Lodahl says this about the scene, "The crusading mind of the scribes and Pharisees experienced crucifixion of sorts, while the woman experienced a resurrection into the grace and new possibilities of God. By deepening; by being willing to get down on ground level, to probe the hearts of those who had the Bible on their side, rather than by manipulating or coercing or bullying or throwing His weight—Jesus brought healing."[8]

Have you learned the "bent down" posture this Advent season? I believe Jesus' challenge to us begins with a crucifixion of our preconceived thoughts and ideas about what it means to be good Christians. The church is full of Pharisees and scribes who need to practice daily the bending down of their thoughts and actions to a God who cannot be contained. It is in that act that we will participate in the deepening of grace, freedom, love, and justice for others and the world.

So how do you practice bending down? Is it a physical act of getting on your knees in prayer? Is it a daily conversation where you verbally acknowledge the Lordship of Jesus? Is it in the service of others?

Prayer

Divine Love, who bends low to look us in the eye, come again to your waiting people and renew our minds so that we may know when we bend down to help a person up that we are helping you. It is for your glory we ask this in the name of our Redeemer, Jesus. Amen.

FRIDAY – DAY 20 – BE BLESSED

Daily Psalm

> *Blessed are those whose ways are blameless,*
> *who walk according to the law of the LORD.*
> *Blessed are those who keep his statutes*
> *and seek him with all their heart—*
> *they do no wrong*
> *but follow his ways.*
> (Psalm 119:1-3)

Acts of Mercy

- Donate your sick days, if your employer allows, to a coworker suffering with a long-term illness or give cash to someone you know is struggling with medical bills. (✉)

- Make a blanket for **Project Linus**, get your hair cut for **Locks of Love**, or send old eyeglasses to the **Lions Club International's Sight Program**. Visit http://www.projectlinus.org, http://locksoflove.org/, or http://www.lionsclubs.org/ for more information.

- Go caroling in a nursing home. (🐾)

Family Devotional

Read Mark 9:33-37.

Blessing for those who follow Jesus has been interpreted in three broad ways. It could be understood as being prestigious, positional, or a responsibility. The prestigious view assumes that we are blessed because we are somehow special or elite. We are blessed because we deserve it based on our relationship with God. And those who are blessed more are closer to God. The positional understanding of blessing assumes that we are blessed and no one else is. Thus we have been blessed with the unique understanding of God and God's plan for

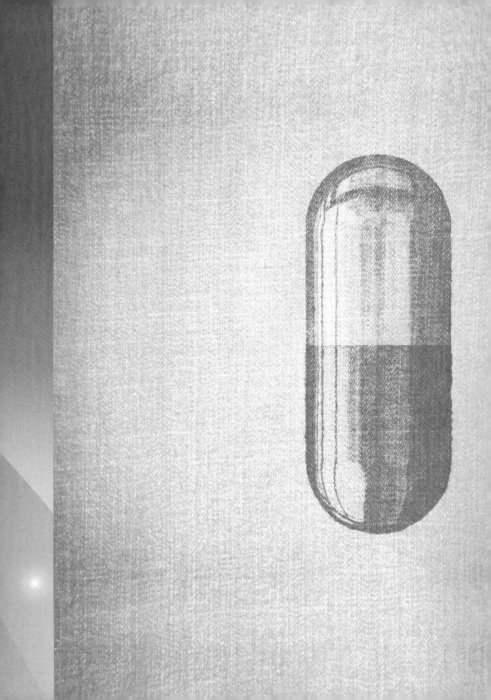

this world. Those that view blessing as a responsibility assume that God has blessed us with a purpose. This view draws from the calling of Abraham who was blessed in order to bless all nations.

The disciples are having a conversation in our passage today about blessing. Specifically, they are arguing about who will be blessed as the greatest in the kingdom of God. They assume that their unique relationship with Jesus the Messiah puts them in a position to receive a well-deserved blessing of honor in God's kingdom.

Jesus sits them down for a talk to expound to them the nature of blessing. In the kingdom, the nature of being blessed is upside down from the world. To be blessed means that you have a great responsibility. Jesus specifically explains that the blessing of being honored as the greatest means that you must be the servant of all in the kingdom.

Then Jesus led a little child into the group and said, "Whoever welcomes one of these little children in my name welcomes me; and whoever welcomes me does not welcome me but the one who sent me" (v. 37). The little child represented one of the weakest groups of people in Jesus' day. In fact, children were treated worse than some animals in that society. So for Jesus to identify with the most vulnerable and abused member of His society is profound. It teaches us that if we follow Jesus, our blessing is found not in prestige or position but in fulfilling our responsibility to welcome the weak and poor in Jesus' name.

Prayer

Holy Trinity, who created us in your loving image, remind us once again that all people are responsible to welcome the weak and poor and help your followers to demonstrate it for the sake of your world and your name we pray. Amen.

SATURDAY – DAY 21 – BE BLESSED

Daily Psalm

> Show me your ways, LORD,
>> teach me your paths.
> Guide me in your truth and teach me,
>> for you are God my Savior,
>> and my hope is in you all day long.
> Remember, LORD, your great mercy and love,
>> for they are from of old.
>>> (Psalm 25:4-6)

Acts of Mercy

- Donate items to a women's shelter. Visit http://www.womenslaw.org for local listings.

- Sign up to mentor an ex-prisoner or help them with practical needs of re-entry. Visit http://www.prisonfellowship.org/get-involved/community/ for more information.

- Participate in a fundraising event, such as Jail and Bail, (🐷) to support **Nazarene Compassionate Ministries CIS Prison Ministry Project** (★). Visit http://ncm.org/projects/acm1739 for more information.

Family Devotional

Read Matthew 21:23-32.

Have you ever just given in or walked away to end a debate with someone? We have probably all encountered someone at one time or another who would argue the opposite of our every point, even to the extent of discrediting their own position. It's impossible to have a meaningful exchange with that type of person because they care more about being right, or you being wrong, than they care about the topic of conversation.

The Pharisees in our passage today are more concerned with being right than being honest. Standing in the temple courts, prepared to start an argument, they throw out a controversial question to Jesus. And Jesus asks them a question to put the conversation ball back in their court. They respond to Jesus' question with "we don't know" because they are bracing themselves for the "what ifs" in the discourse that would follow. They cared more about how they would be perceived than what the truth actually was.

Imagine a contestant on *Who Wants to be a Millionaire* who won't take the plunge. The host asks, "Is that your final answer?" and the contestant responds, "I don't know." At some point we have to lock in our answer. Even if our answer is wrong we have to own it. We have to live and learn. If we remain in a state of uncertainty, always playing it safe, aren't we being lukewarm?

We have the blessing and responsibility to come to the Truth and share Him with others. We must actively search for the truth and live it out. As we encounter others during the acts of mercy, may we be honest in motive, discourse and action.

Prayer

Word of Truth, who spoke reality into existence, breathe on us once again so that we might know truth through the transforming work of your Spirit we ask. Amen.

SUNDAY – DAY 22

Reflection on Matthew 1:18-25

"The virgin will conceive and give birth to a son, and **they will call him Immanuel**" (which means "God with us"). (Matthew 1:25)

Be Amazed

We live in a world filled with miracles of technology. Humans landed on the moon and decades later space travel is common place. We mapped the human genome and daily unlock the mystery of the human mind with fMRI. We've developed computational equipment that once fit in a room and now fits in the palm of our hands. We communicate in video, audio, photos, and texts throughout the globe at such a rapid rate that we truly do have the world at our fingertips. In the flood of such technological innovation our senses are drowning in a sea of amazing. We are so amused by our own creativity that we need a kind of imagination defibrillator to shock the dysrhythmia of our passions with the awe-inspiring reality of God.

Amazing Faithfulness TO God

We need to go no further to find our shock factor than an unassuming carpenter in 1st century Palestine. Joseph is a young Jewish guy whose arranged marriage to a teen girl in the village has taken an unexpected turn. He finds out that she is pregnant and he knows it isn't by him. He knows that infidelity is always unjust, but he also values obedience to God above all else. Joseph knows that the God of his ancestors is a God that requires mercy and not sacrifice. So Joseph models justice tempered by mercy when he decides to break off the engagement quietly.

This is an amazingly righteous and loving decision for a young guy to make in his day. Add to that the fact no parents are present in the story. Joseph and Mary are both young and their marriage, if following 1st century Jewish customs, was almost certainly an arranged marriage. The decision to break off the arrangement would have had to come by one of the heads of the family. But we don't see them in the story. So we must assume that Joseph either had to insist his father allow him to break off the engagement quietly or that Joseph doesn't have any head of the household to speak for him. In a culture that valued the wisdom of age, Joseph's youth makes his piety all the more amazing.

If the story stopped there we would have a great story of a holy follower of God which would be a good moral story to tell your kids. But the truly amazing part of the story hasn't even happened yet. God intervenes in this situation. Not because God is attempting to turn Joseph away from an ungodly or evil path but rather to call Joseph deeper into the unfolding salvation story.

A messenger of God appears in a dream to Joseph. There were three instructions given by the messenger to Joseph. First he is to take Mary as his wife. Second, he was not to consummate the marriage until after she gives birth. And finally, Joseph is to call the baby "Jesus," for He will save His people from their sins. The first instruction would cause Joseph and Mary public shame and possibly being disowned by their family. The second instruction would require extreme restraint on both their part. And the final instruction signaled that God was up to an Exodus-like rescue mission and that Joseph, Mary, and the unborn child were invited to take an immediate role in this mission. Joseph awoke from his sleep to go and do what God had revealed to him.

Amazing Faithfulness OF God

Matthew 1:23 is a thumbnail sketch of Matthew's understanding of Jesus as the Son of God. For Matthew, Jesus functions as the mediator of God's presence as the "Son of God." The church has reflected on this amazing revelation of the incarnation of God who unites with humanity.

The incarnation is the basis for Jesus Christ being the representative for all humanity. Being born a human, Christ could identify with humanity completely or in such a way that no aspect of humanity was overshadowed or overpowered by His deity or vice versa. He could represent humanity before God allowing Him to be the one who would justify, sanctify, and redeem all humanity. Thus, Christ

uniting with all humanity according to the flesh was the beginning of the work of salvation, which would be completed in His life, death, and resurrection.

Since Christ already completed the work of justification, sanctification, and redemption in His life, death, and resurrection, when we are united with Him according to the Spirit we are justified, sanctified and redeemed. Therefore, we can affirm the writer of Hebrews who wrote, "...by one sacrifice he has made perfect forever those who are being made holy" (10:12-14). This points to the reality that those who are reborn by the Spirit, and thus united with Christ, are saved and continue the path of growing in Christlikeness.

We, the Church, who are awake to the amazing revelation that God is with us, are called to go forth and be witnesses to this reality. In faithfulness to God, we are to be the body of Christ and announce the good news that our Christ has come and He will come again. We go out to bear fruit which reveals God's presence. And we reach out to all as the least of all servants in the kingdom so that all may know the amazing reality that our God is Emmanuel.

Acts of Piety

- Journal about what you've experienced during the your acts of mercy.

- Testify in church or on social networks about how He has blessed you in your attempt to be His hands and feet.

- Pray for God to show you how to continue the Advent beyond this Advent season.

MONDAY – DAY 23 – BE AMAZED

Daily Psalm

> I will remember the deeds of the LORD;
>   yes, I will remember your miracles of long ago.
> I will consider all your works
>   and meditate on all your mighty deeds."
> Your ways, God, are holy.
>   What god is as great as our God?
> You are the God who performs miracles;
>   you display your power among the peoples.
>   (Psalm 77:11-14)

Acts of Mercy

- Pay for the car behind you in the drive-thru. (✉)

- Treat a friend to a meal.

- Donate canned goods to a local homeless shelter or food pantry. (🐾)

Family Devotional

Read Luke 1:26-38.

Our passage today is a story about the impossible. It is the story of the angel's announcement to Mary. There are several basic impossibilities in this story. A pregnant teenager is having a child and yet is a virgin. Impossible! Her betrothed is following through on the marriage when he discovers she is pregnant. Impossible! They are avoiding death when the neighbors hear the news. Impossible!

This is a story of biblical impossibilities. What are the impossibilities in our world? What would you label "impossible" in your life? Peace in our world. Impossible! No way! Restoring broken relationships with certain family members? Impossible! They'll never change. Our church reaching our surrounding community and making our world

different? Impossible! Won't happen! Healing past hurts in our lives; a relative or friend entering a relationship with Christ; breaking an addiction; overcoming disappointments? Impossible!

How can the impossible become possible? Look at Luke 1:35. The power of the Most High will overshadow her. The image may bring to mind the cloud in Exodus 40:38, representing the presence and power of God. It reminds us of how, in Genesis 1:2, God's Spirit hovered over the waters in creation (although it is a different word it has a similar feel).

How can the impossible become possible? The power of God is going to be released into the life of Mary. God is going to act on her behalf. God is going to speak His name—Son of the Most High—into the world. He is going to say the word . . . "possible." When the Most High God says the word, the impossible becomes possible.

This Advent season you've spent your days performing acts of mercy. These acts may have seemed insignificant in the face of the needs in the world. The good news is that providing for the needs is not impossible for God. We wait in Advent with the hope that the God of the impossible will come quickly and wipe away every need. Until that time, we hope and faithfully follow the God who makes the impossible, possible.

Prayer

Almighty God, who saves by your might right hand, come quickly to save those who are in desperate need of food, water, and warmth for your glory we pray. Amen.

TUESDAY – DAY 24 – BE AMAZED

Daily Psalm

I will declare your name to my people;
in the assembly I will praise you.
You who fear the Lord, praise him!
All you descendants of Jacob, honor him!
Revere him, all you descendants of Israel!
For he has not despised or scorned
the suffering of the afflicted one;
he has not hidden his face from him
but has listened to his cry for help.
(Psalm 22:22-24)

Acts of Mercy

- Tape enough quarters to a vending machine for a drink. (✉)

- Skip the Caramel Macchiato or Big Gulp® and give the money saved ($) to the **Nazarene Compassionate Ministries Global Clean Water Fund** (★). Visit http://ncm.org/projects/acm1423 for more information.

- Pass out juice boxes at a playground or water bottles at the gym. (🍃, ✉)

Family Devotional

Read Luke 1:46-56.

In the beautiful words the Christian world has come to know as "The Magnificat" (so named for the translation of the Latin word for "magnify"), the humble and unassuming young woman from Nazareth praises God for her blessing and utters the most revolutionary words.

Through her, the Holy Spirit speaks of how God's divine plan is to bring down the mighty and lift up the lowly—to feed the hungry and poor!

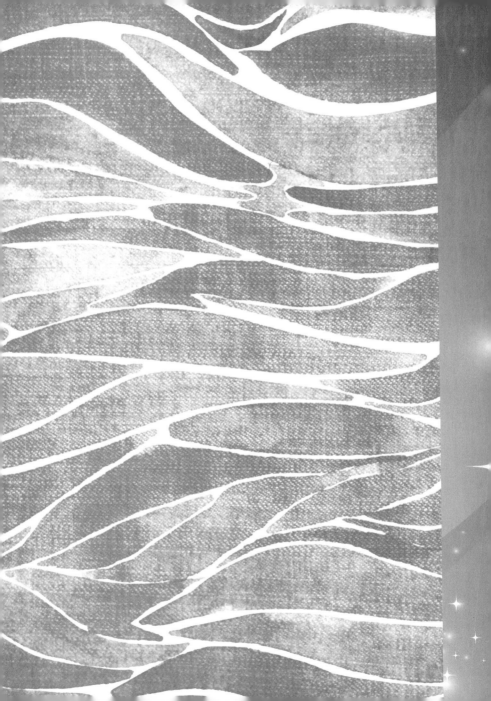

"He has performed mighty deeds with his arm; he has scattered those who are proud in their inmost thoughts. He has brought down rulers from their thrones but has lifted up the humble. He has filled the hungry with good things but has sent the rich away empty" (Luke 1:51-53).

As well as news that must be shared and celebrated, this is news that must be lived. When God comes with blessing, there is a specific promise that wrong will be made right and injustice will give way to justice.

As we celebrate this wonderful joyous day, our hearts are drawn to the day God came with blessing through a gentle mother and tender child in a tiny village across the oceans. And in the words that are "joy to the world" there is a promise to all who have been "left out."

This season our hearts will also be drawn to give something to our Lord who has need of our joyful obedience. The good news is news to live as well as to celebrate. It may be difficult to do during this time of year when we find ourselves so wrapped up in our family, friends and blessings. But we must look around at those who have need of God's good news even on this day. There are so many in our world who are not included in the blessings we enjoy. They long for the time when God will exalt the lowly and fill the hungry with good things.

Prayer

King of All, who exalts the lowly, may your Spirit go forth to fill your people once again so that poor hear and experience the good news of your coming kingdom. We ask this in the name of your Son. Amen.

WEDNESDAY – CHRISTMAS DAY

Family Devotional

Read Luke 2:1-20.

Celebrate is from a Latin word that means "to frequent." And the past usage of the word indicated that you repeated some practice over and over again. The point of the repetition was to keep a memory or event alive in your imagination and daily life. This is what we do when we celebrate Communion. And it is what we do when we celebrate Christmas.

I suggest that what we celebrate in Christmas is not merely the birth of a baby. I think the reason we celebrate Christmas is that God has broken into His creation by becoming like His creation. The incarnation is the profound mystery that keeps us repeating the story, the gift-giving, and all of the many traditions of Christmas. Deep inside our practices of Christmas is this enduring prayer from the prophet Isaiah:

"Oh, that you would rend the heavens and come down, that the mountains would tremble before you! For when you did awesome things that we did not expect, you came down, and the mountains trembled before you" (Isaiah 64:1, 3).

And it truly is an awesome thing that our God has done. He came to the seemingly insignificant, yet faithful ones of His chosen people. A teenage girl and a young guy, who were from a good-for-nothing town called Nazareth, are at the epicenter of God's amazing action of being born a human. It was not enough that He submit himself to be born into the royal courts which are not good enough for our God; He bent so low that He turned the world order upside down. And it is to this day that we celebrate the reality that the Son of God, "who being in the very nature God, didn't consider equality with God something to be used to his own advantage; rather, he made himself nothing by taking the very nature of a servant, being made in human likeness" (Philippians 2:6-7).